30 Days Dry

Robert Eric Shoemaker

Thought Collection Publishing
Chicago

THOUGHT COLLECTION PUBLISHING
P.O. Box 35192
Elmwood Park, Illinois, 60707
www.ThoughtCollection.org

Editing by Troy Cabida
Design by Kat Lahr
All Illustrations Copyright © 2015 by Susanne Wawra

First Edition, 2015

ISBN-10: 0996663509
ISBN-13: 978-0-9966635-0-2

We hope you enjoy this book from Thought Collection Publishing. Our goal
is to provide thought-provoking books to promote the practice of thinking.

* Researching Humanity's Thoughts *

Dedicated to
my cheerleader, my mentor, and
my spiritual guide:
my father, Ed Shoemaker.

Special thanks to
Kat, Troy, Susanne, and Thought Collection for
supporting my habit.

Contents

CONTENTS

30 Days Dry

———— ◆ ————

Day one.

*Viciousness in the bedroom! I am as good as my clock.
Sleep beckons: there is room here.

I shrink myself. Into a wrapper, aluminum ball electrified,
waiting for the switch in the bathtub, half full of tepid smelling water—
salts at hand. Positive and negative they say is like jumping a car,
and on medication, it is more like a miniature car zipping from carpet
square to square.

I shrink myself, a doctored prescription I wrote at my sewing desk,
zipping up dead moths and one living moth inside who eats the
others. I swallow it whole and the moths zip around inside my
stomach-sac. Gall and dust mingle on my insides.

I shrink myself, lest I melt away in an electrical embrace, an
ice cube in the flame of the showerhead, tapping on my shoulders
where I sit down and hope for the best— the water up to my chin,
I dump the salts in, fire up my battery, blow a fuse— hot! The fizzle of
my melted brain seeping out my nostrils to the jumping bean water
inside me; the interior melts away
I float above myself
the moth is free to hunt other live moths.

I shrink myself, and the lights are blown.

Day two.

Observation: Had a good first half of day. Must work on second half.

I make like a clock and
Run! My-mirror-me shakes
Through, blows a .5, cracks a
Frown and has how-to!
What a run, he thinks, as I
Paper copy-up walls with
Layers of cardboard.
You can smell dead trees.

Day three.

*Bi as in two poles like that penguin place ain't no joke, Smith.***

Much being the worthy application
of palm oil to the olive,
as is the cause to the root,
as the foot to that throb you nurse—
called a pinched nerve.
Much the root of the hand
the bone, the radius anatomy
is there not a diameter pi
the impossible number as is the
nervous throb and tic you
apply oil to, you nurse.
Being the ulna completes the circuit
as a compulsive liar
Being the root cause of death:
oh, you'll feel better soon,
it all grows back.
Much is lasting
the instants you nurse
and their radii.

*Feelin good workout post-traumatic syndrome
**Feelin good grocery post-static syndrome
***Feelin good work time post-traumatic blues

Day four.

Snow
And Lots of It.
Shake It!
...
glitter
dangled by angels.

Day five.

Do I see in that alley there a wide-hipped monster
savoring his claws at me—
Whispering here here here
Knock knock
His or her top hat is a red beacon whirring and I am a fox without
a pole-arm.

Day six.

Vestigial rat scents:
feeling them leave me, they are like the carrot.
They swell as they grow deeper and deeper putting out little hairs
little teeth to suck up the nutriment
the soil closing in around them, making it darker and
harder to breathe, a chore to breathe—
eventually filling in the space the carrot left.

Day seven.

Trying titles.
Really ruining the week's worth of wine.
What was that again, that classic line, in the old style?

Recommendation: Read something, twice daily. Repeat as needed.

Day eight.

***Feeling bad for missing workout post-traumatic syndrome.
*Recommendation: Regression is a bitch. Work past it.

Day nine.

TEMPTATION, knock with a wide blue eyed face. His name
Last Night Lucas and he appeared to me as a dream fighter with
the palest of faces,
the largest of palms; I brushed
past him with a martini in hand, thickening my body
for the impact. I felt
the veins brush skin through the martini haze, and the
little soldiers
on his arm
meet my bicep and stand
at arms his head turned,

but I was
Already Gone. will I
be a PHANTOM
to him
too
?

Day ten.

Did I mistake myself,
or is that a hypocrite on the other side of the mirror?

*Suggestion:
monstrous gauntlets
much being the application
of pro-secco.*

Day eleven.

What so makes you think that I want to be a part of something
called *body pump?**

Your crass eyes and tongue clicking gawp
at my diminishing-but-not-fast-enough waist,
my arms (like atrophied fish eyes)
struggle for what will soon be lost.
Leave me below a lowly
but healthy worm-let.

Missed workout post-traumatic stress binge

Day twelve.

I chase my tail; the poet's anthologizing momentum is circular and cyclical, my tail of iambic hexametric rhyming Rothenbergs and Spicers in my tea so that I stay awake as long as that chart with those people who were geniuses supposedly woke up so early, like six, and wrote at that time?

I can hardly sleep at that time I cannot tell how to awake that part of me now at eleven and post meridian much less at six.

I swallow my tail, my ancestors, like bell jars and butterflies, on buttered bread, like thought foxes stinking, like yawp and barbarian kings, like stones leaves doors, like hereditary illness, like Geryon's wings, like Circe and her pigs, like only rock like no water, like a how town,

like hwaet!

Listen to me: I have a voice to speak I can articulate my own I have internal rhythms I speak language like a rocket

not like a wind up monkey like a photograph I'll capture

the soul of the world and put it up for you to read in some gallery somewhere

and you'll say isn't that nice, a puppy.

*Recommendation: Read something, anything.**
**Rinse and repeat.

Day thirteen.

Round and round,
I can hear
What I have written in my
Jack is a good boy.
Round and
Round, I can hear what
I have written in my Jack
Is a good boy. round
And round I
Can hear what
I have written in my Jack
Is a good boy. round and
Round I can hear what I have
Written in my Jack is a good
Boy round and round
I can hear what I have written in my
Jack is a good round and round
I hear what I have written in my good boy
Round and round,

**Strongly worded text: sleep is a good mistress.*

Day fourteen.

Today's the day and I'm feeling sluggish.
Your past savors its fingers at me, long and iambic-jointed:

A fine film, brown and musty, coats your paw
as you sit slightly dejected across
the room, avoiding her gaze. Once, you shook
hands with all her friends, held tight as she took

your damp spongy limb into her paw, kissed
you wetly, little lips. Some nights she missed
you when leaving home, shifting to another;
her new friends, leaving you with her mother.

And you gather dust and must remain, still.

**Strongly worded recommendation letter:
The wheels on the bus go round and round.
Leave behind the strongest image of yourself.

Day fifteen.

Wasabi Pea Delight
in What I Took From My Cabinet
Left like a Fly.

Delight ain't What is Left
In My Cabinet:
Wasabi Pea

.

Back to square one.

Day sixteen.

Redemption is all day every day: submission day.
Not submissive, not like a rule, not a quietude,
but a submission,
as in, I submit myself to your jurisdiction,
I send you
a piece of my ear in a manila envelope
and you tell me if you can transplant.
Redemption is
Submission like
Round and round, we go!
The cult of rejection:
Fear is an animal,
not submissive, like a rule; He is quiet, on cat feet,
He sends you
a piece of his fur, and you stick it on your own,
and it meshes sometimes,
or it don't
and you have something like a rule, like rejection, like a Poem.
Redemption is thus something like submission.

Day seventeen.

Is redemption?

Puppetting myself.

Is redemption
puppetting myself?

Is
Redemption
puppeting

Myself?

Is
Redemption
Puppetting myself?

Is
Redemption
Puppetting
Myself
?

Personal Goal #1: Medicate.

Day eighteen.

I spent that day
as if it were distant already.

I had a panic attack
and I rolled my eyes in bed round and round in my head
I slept in a coma of blankets
puppy, puppet, he is here.

I had a manic attack,
Productivity like a Lion
roars I spent that hour
Here and that hour
as if I were finishing.

I am writing a children's song
and so I drink.

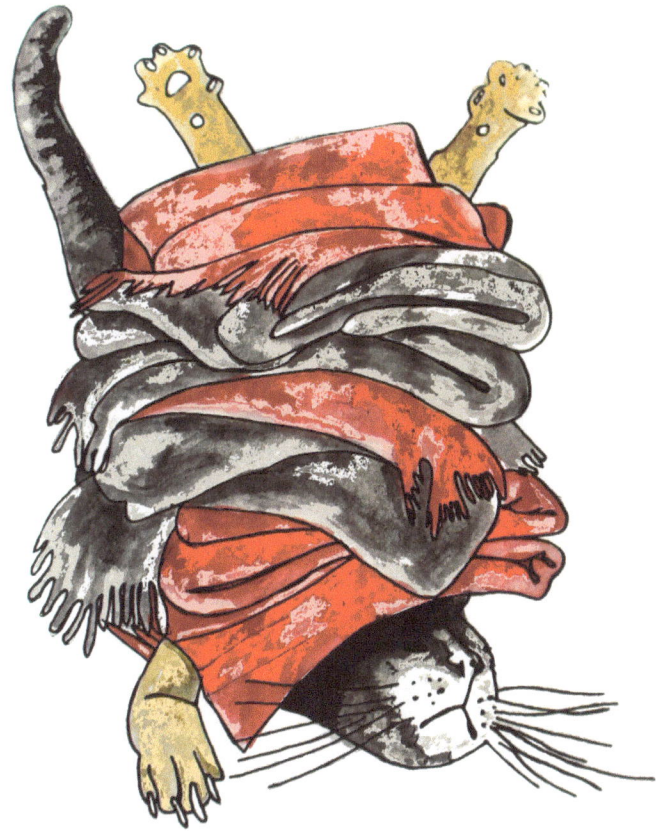

Day nineteen.

I was out, all day, in the city.

What is the artistic balance of work and art? I am struggling to know
what the difference really is between doing what one wants
to do and doing what one has to do and why they are not the same
thing can they be the same thing?

I am thinking of a number between 1 and 2 do you know what it is
can I evaluate your intelligence based on a question so dumb
can you answer quickly enough and if so will you be qualified
for me to give you this job?

What is the pragmatic balance of work and art?
The university is an academic playground but the universe is
absolutely
not for the academic it is for the work force working man
it does not require the skills to make an argument
only to have an argument
it does not require the skills to craft an idea
only to craft a burrito: like a burrito, the recommendation letter
is folded neatly and placed in an envelope with care,
then heated up and ding it comes out and someone somewhere eats
it and is satisfied or has a stomach-ache.

Why I who has the luxury to make this decision?

Day twenty.

I put my phone by the coffee pot
To Wake Myself Up.
I set a timer on the coffee pot
so that it is operating
when I am asleep
and when it is done
ding
my phone wakes Me up
and I have to walk to the kitchen
to turn it off
and then I reward myself with coffee.
I read this on Facebook:
"it is the only way to get me out of bed"

****Recommendation:
The wheels on the bus
go round and round
#1 medicate
#2 optimize*

Day twenty-one.

Have You
a history of Self-mutilation?
a history of suicidal thoughts— or feelings?
You are telling— look at that face!
just look at it, You are rat-faced.
have You, Yourself
incense? You write it,
do You feel it?
i smell it on You, You
rat
like sandalwood more like sea-grass
Your greens grow like spread seed
the soil unyielding unhappy
have You
Your history of Self-incarceration?

i find myself knowing You, despite reservations.

Day twenty-two.

Am I slowly killing my cat?
He is
passing strange
like a ship at sea
that looks both ways, slowly, its foghorn constantly blowing.

He wants to stay
in the empty tub.

I understand the feeling,

so should I get out my salts?

Day twenty-three.

I am a band of horses
at Cliff's Edge
I sip a cup of lemon herb chamomile
and bubble my toes.

I am accepting a job,
a working horse
outside my pen, I run!

Round and round,
my mirror-me cracks a
smile, has how-to!

*Recommendation:
spiked coffee
is not for coworkers.

Day twenty-four.

A vanish play time
gone wrong
bad like eggs
Eurydice had a cough
he thought it was to get attention
and Orpheus looked back.

*Shared text:
Would Orpheus' song be like a horse's or like a rat's?
**Goal: Read more.

Day twenty-five.

The job looking tough
the colt bucks.

An old friend calls
Ohio for lunch?

Rat-faced wanderer, you deny suggestion
and peel away your mirror.

Put it back on:
beneath you are too angular.

Day twenty-six.

I've always thought of hobos as prophets,
like the one next to me in Starbucks, reading the free papers.
Doing the crossword, is she unlocking a code—
will she withdraw from her plastic grocery bag
bones to spell history,
is she feeding her augury in the park?
Does she surround herself with prophecies and amulets by stuffing
her coat;
is she mumbling a hex on anyone who looks at her funny?

Her fire in her can is her cauldron
what is she thinking when she lies on the exhaust vents and
shuts her eyes?

Day twenty-seven.

Dread
Dread
Red
Dread
Fills my eyes and my hairtips.

Not a stallion, nor a colt,
my foal-mane stiff, it gives me away.

Recommendation letter, ctnd.
"Nothing is forever."

Day twenty-eight.

Somehow, I chose both to shave and to start work
during a blizzard.
Coincidence?

I step inside the warmth of the coach house where my friends' smiles
and stripes
welcome by small talk,
looking away, thinking, will I be grey
GREY
like a rotten rotten peach?
I don't want to mold in a corner,
but the blizzard storms on and I keep thinking of how grey
snow really is

.

Day twenty-nine.

Monday, the earliest day, breeding me out of my cozy hovel
and smacking my new-babe ass until I cry out
"Fuck it's cold,
someone turn off the snow."

And wouldn't you know it, I can't start until Wednesday.

Two more days of cold Panera coffee,
Two more days to write before descending into the Man's maw.
Will I spend them well, or just crying out, "Hark, unclean!?"

Your top hat creeps at me in eyelets, sharp and round and small. I
can't look
too close
or your claws will claw me,
but I wonder: is poetry worth the pain?

If [not] winter,
No pain is
*

Day thirty.

Round and round
My Jack ain't no good boy but
The Cabinet Is empty

I think I understand this time.

There's a rhythm
It comes in waves
consistent
yet shrinking

Dropping a coin into a pot of boiling water
doesn't make an impression.

Can you spell history? I can.

Afterword

No son wants to hear his father tell him that he drinks too much- especially while sitting at the Olive Garden.
It really wrecks the serenity.
But it also wrecked my delusion that I was "okay" at the time.
I was thinking, what recent college grad doesn't have a few problems? As long as they're addressing them, it's fine- right?

I began "30 Days Dry" in a vain attempt to answer the question, "What is the artistic balance of work and art?" or even more vainly, "Can I stop drinking long enough to care?" and ended trying to answer, "Why does art matter right now when work and stability are [arguably] more important?"

I struggled through 30 days of self-improvement, and failed in some ways, but learned as I changed (not grew). I learned something(s), and failed to learn others. Cycles developed, habits were formed or examined or annihilated, and the impartment of knowledge began.

My cycles are nothing like yours, but I hope to at least make a dent in mine and an impression on yours. Hopefully, this guide is at least self-helpful.

After all, I'm just another one.

-RES

About The Artists

Robert Eric Shoemaker is a Chicago based poet-playwright, director, and arts journalist.

Eric's theatrical work has been seen at Gorilla Tango Theatre, City Lit Theatre, American Theater Company, 3 Brothers Theatre, Mary-Arrchie Theatre Company, and others.

He was awarded the 2014 Olga and Paul Menn Foundation Prize for Best Play for his musical PLATH/HUGHES, as well as a 2015 DCASE Individual Artist Program grant from the City of Chicago for his project "LORCA IN AMERICA".

In addition to making theatre, Eric is an arts journalist and poet published in Newcity, Evanston Now, Rollick Magazine, the Chicago After Dark Anthology, Literature Emitting Diodes and the Pulitzer Center on Crisis Reporting.

This is Eric's first book of poetry.

Eric is a graduate with honors from the University of Chicago, where he was Artistic Director of the Classical Entertainment Society.

Follow his work at reshoemaker.com.

Susanne Wawra is a German visual artist and poet based in Dublin, Ireland. Susanne holds a MA in English and Communication & Media from the University of Leipzig, Germany. After an exploration of work life in an international big name company, she decided to swap a secure career for life as an artist.

The human condition is a recurring theme in her work. Particularly, she explores vulnerability and Weltschmerz through painting, collage and video. Her work has been exhibited in Ireland and the UK, Germany, Italy and the United States.

Even though English is not her mother tongue, it is her preferred medium for poetry. Her first collection "Schizo-Poetry - Fragments of Mind" with co-writer Kevin Nolan was published in May 2015. Recent journal publications include Galway Review, Weyfarers, Valve Journal, Skylight 47 and Boyne Berries. More info at www.susannewawra.com.

About The Series

Thought Collection Publishing's 30 Days... series challenges artists to write consecutively for 30 days on a specific area of study, reflection, or expertise. In return they would personally experience something amazing. The manuscripts in the 30 Days... series are all personal journeys that expand life perspectives.

Thought Collection Publishing is an indie publisher supporting social change through our narrative nonfiction publications. Ten percent of sales from "30 Days Dry" goes to support the Howard Brown Health Center's Recovering With Pride substance use program.

Join the publisher's contact list to stay informed about projects and other books in this series at: eepurl.com/CuL35.

WWW.THOUGHTCOLLECTION.ORG

The **HUMAN THOUGHT PROJECT**™ for
Thought Collection Publishing

Publishing For Social Change